(OULD YOU EVER?

Build a Time Machine

By Dr. David Darling

DILLON PRESS, INC.
Minneapolis, Minnesota 55415

Library of Congress Cataloging-in-Publication
Data

Darling, David J.
    Could you ever build a time machine? /
David Darling.
        p.   cm.
    Includes bibliographical references (p.   ).
    Summary: Examines the nature of time,
time machines, and the possibility of time
travel, discussing Einstein's relativity theory
and the chances of time travelers from the
future visiting us in the present.
    ISBN 0-87518-456-1 (lib. bind.)
    1. Time—Juvenile literature.   2. Time
travel—Juvenile literature.   [1. Time.
2. Time travel.]   I. Title.
QB209.5.D37   1991
530.1'1—dc20   90-3961
                                          CIP
                                           AC

Dillon Press, Inc., 242 Portland Avenue South
Minneapolis, Minnesota 55415

Printed in the United States of America
1 2 3 4 5 6 7 8 9 10 00 99 98 97 96 95 94 93 92 91

Photographic Acknowledgments

The photographs are reproduced through
the courtesy of the California Institute of
Technology/Carnegie Institution; Kalm-
bach Publishing Co./*Odyssey* magazine;
Kitt Peak National Observatory; National
Aeronautics and Space Administration;
National Optical Astronomy Observatories;
Mark Paternostro; Betts Anderson, Wm.
Chris Brown, H.H. Thomas III/Unicorn
Stock Photos; U.S. Space and Rocket Cen-
ter/U.S. Space Camp®, U.S. Space Acad-
emy®, NASA Visitor Center; Science
VU-LBL, VU-CBS/Visuals Unlimited.

METRIC CONVERSION CHART To Find Approximate Equivalents		
WHEN YOU KNOW:	**MULTIPLY BY:**	**TO FIND:**
TEMPERATURE degrees Fahrenheit (minus 32)	0.56	degrees Celsius
LENGTH		
feet	30.48	centimeters
yards	0.91	meters
miles	1.61	kilometers
MASS (weight)		
pounds	0.45	kilograms
tons	0.91	metric tons
VOLUME		
cubic yards	0.77	cubic meters
AREA		
acres	0.41	hectares
square miles	2.59	square kilometers
CAPACITY		
gallons	3.79	liters

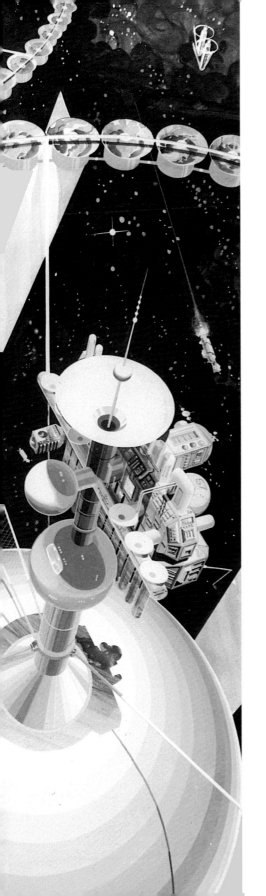

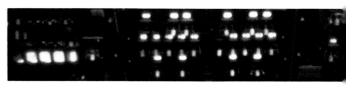

Contents

The Challenge • *4*

About Time • *7*

It's Yesterday Once More • *19*

Shortcuts to the Future • *27*

Black Holes and Time Tunnels • *41*

Hands On • *56*

Glossary • *57*

Index • *60*

The Challenge

In the movie, *Back to the Future*, hero Marty McFly travels back in time to November 5, 1955. At that point in time, he meets his parents-to-be as high school students. For a while it seems as if Marty's presence might change the past so that his mom and dad will not fall in love. And if they never go on to marry and have children, how could Marty ever be born to travel in the past? Fortunately, this remaking of his family history is avoided in the nick of time. Still, when Marty arrives back in the 1980s, he finds his family to be somewhat different than he had remembered it!

The idea of traveling through time has been explored in many books and films over the years. For instance, in *The Time Machine*, the English author H.G. Wells tells of a remarkable journey into the year 802,701. In this short story, human beings have been

Imagine what it would be like to travel back in time to the age of dinosaurs.

divided into two very different races—the gentle, childlike "eloi" and the terrible "morlocks." The morlocks live underground. There they work with machinery and provide for the daily needs of the eloi, who dwell on the surface. But the morlocks also treat the eloi like fatted cattle, taking a few of them each night for food.

Other writers have whisked their heroes and heroines into a more hopeful future. Still others have described trips into the past, to the year of the French Revolution or the long-ago age of dinosaurs. But could time travel ever become more than just an author's fantasy? Could it ever happen in the real world?

In one sense, we travel through time every moment of our lives. A few seconds into the future, you will be reading the words of the next sentence in this book. Now it is happening, and you are actually reading them. But now, they are no longer in the future, or the present, but the past.

You have just done a little time-traveling of your own!

Yet this everyday kind of movement through time is not very

exciting. What we really mean by time travel is being able to jump back into the past or forward into the future, as far or as quickly as we like. Will that ever be possible? Could you, in fact, ever build a time machine?

People have developed many ways to travel through space, but not through time. Here, U.S. Space Academy students take their turn as commander and pilot inside the cockpit of a space shuttle mockup at the U.S. Space Camp Training Center in Huntsville, Alabama.

About Time

Try a simple experiment. Make sure first that you are wearing a watch. Now, walk forward and backward, to the right and to the left. Walk faster, or run, in any direction you like. Jump up and down. Move however you wish, for as long as you wish. Check the time on your watch against a clock that has remained at rest, both before and after your period of exercise. What do you notice?

The results of this experiment are clear. They show that while you have freedom to move around in space, you have no control at all over your motion through time. Despite all your efforts, your watch will not appear to have gained or lost any time as compared with the clock that did not move.

Yet, the more you think about it, the stranger that seems. After all, people today can quickly cover huge distances in jet aircraft. They can explore both on and below the Earth's surface. Astronauts have even traveled as far away as the Moon. We can move about in space almost as we please. Yet no one has ever managed to jump even one second forward into the future or back into the past.

We are all forced, it seems, to move through time at the same rate and in the same direction. It is as if we were passengers together on a train. All we can see is the ever-changing scenery of the present moment through the side windows. The view through the driver's window at what is to come, and through the back window from the caboose at what has already gone by, is blocked from us. Or is it?

Gone But Not Forgotten
The human brain has an astonishing ability to recall scenes and sounds in great detail, even if they happened many years ago. Because of this, we can relive the past in our minds. We can even recreate

Where Our Calendar Came From

People have not always had a strong interest in the past or the future. Long ago, they did not need to keep an exact record of the changing seasons. But when men and women began to settle and depend heavily on farming, they needed to form a calendar. If the crops were not sown and harvested at the right time of year, there would not be enough food for people to eat. This was especially important in ancient Egypt where life revolved around the annual flooding of the river Nile.

Built thousands of years ago, the Pyramids of Giza in Egypt rise from the desert by the Nile River.

The Egyptians noticed that the Nile floods came at about the same time each year. They always started around the day when the bright star Sirius appeared on the horizon just before sunrise. As a result, this day was taken to mark the start of the Egyptian year. The year was then split up into 12 months of 30 days. Five extra days were added at the end to make 365 in all. Using this scheme, the Egyptian calendar kept reasonably in step with the seasons.

But the time it takes the Earth to go once around the Sun is not exactly 365 days. It is really about 365 and one-fourth days. Every four years, then, the Egyptian calendar fell one day behind in relation to the seasons. Under the Roman emperor Julius Caesar, adjustments were made to the Egyptian calendar to allow for a "leap year." This was a year with one extra day (February 29) every four years. Caesar also shortened and lengthened some of the months. His successor, Augustus, made more changes. (The months July and August are named in honor of these two important figures.) Finally, in 1582, Pope Gregory XIII announced some slight corrections that created the Gregorian calendar we still use today.

parts of the past that other people may have missed by writing about them or drawing pictures from memory.

This talent for remembering and passing on knowledge is one of the reasons human beings have been able to make such remarkable progress. Throughout human history, people have made many great discoveries, inventions, and works of art. The past has been preserved through books, paintings, sculptures, and music.

But more recently, humans have developed other, more accurate ways of bringing the past back to life. Since the middle of the nineteenth century, cameras have allowed events to be captured on film. Through photographs, we can see how things really were at a particular place and time.

Movie cameras have given us even more power to recreate the past. Since their invention around the start of this century, they have recorded many of the world's greatest events. Today, from World War I battles to astronauts on the Moon, these can be viewed over and over again. People who had not even been born at the time can see glimpses of the world from more than 50 years ago.

Not only sights, but also sounds can now be replayed with complete accuracy. Following the invention of the phonograph in 1877, our ability to record and replay sounds has developed at a rapid pace. Today, with hand-held TV sound cameras and

10

A young person uses a camera to capture and preserve an image from a moment in time. ▌

Modern inventions
such as camcorders
and video recorders
allow people to
store and replay
sounds and mov-
ing pictures from
the past.

video recorders, we can capture, in precise detail, sounds and moving pictures from the everyday world. For example, people now routinely record the birth of their children or family Christmas celebrations on videotape. Then, years later, the tape can be shown on a television set to bring back memories of that time. In a sense, the TV screen becomes a window on the past.

Times Around the World

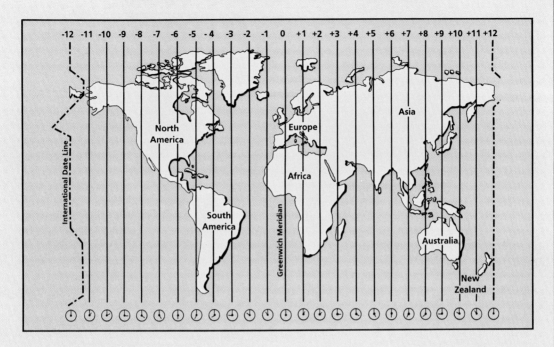

As schools break for lunch in Los Angeles, children in New York are already heading home for the day. The United States (including Hawaii and Alaska) spans seven different time zones, with an hour between each zone. There is a three-hour difference between states on the west and east coasts.

For most purposes, times around the world are set according to Greenwich mean time (GMT). Greenwich is a place near London through which the line of zero degrees longitude passes. Lines of longitude are imaginary lines drawn over the Earth's surface between the north and south poles. There are 360 degrees of longitude—180 to the west of Greenwich and 180 to the east.

To the west of Greenwich, local time is behind Greenwich time. To the east, it is ahead. The time changes by one hour for every 15 degrees of longitude. For example, New York City, which is about 75 degrees west of Greenwich, is five hours behind GMT.

The only difficulty with this system occurs on the opposite side of the world from Greenwich. On the line of longitude that is both 180 degrees to the west of Greenwich and 180 degrees to the east, there has to be a sudden jump from one day to the next. This line is known as the International Date Line. It passes more or less down the middle of the Pacific Ocean. A ship sailing east from Japan to the United States has to move its clocks back by a full 24 hours when it crosses the International Date Line. Going the other way, clocks have to be moved forward by one whole day.

The Past All Around

When we look at photographs, listen to recorded music, or watch homemade family videos, we are 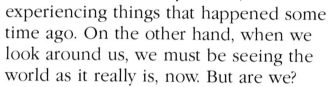 experiencing things that happened some time ago. On the other hand, when we look around us, we must be seeing the world as it really is, now. But are we?

The sounds you are hearing at this moment come from a thousandth of a second in the past for every foot they traveled to reach your ears. You do not hear them instantly because sound moves through air at about 1,000 feet per second. During a thunderstorm, for instance, the rumble from a lightning flash three miles away will not reach you for 15 seconds.

What is true of sound is also true of light. But light travels about a million times faster than sound, or 186,282 miles per second. This is such an enormous speed that the light from everyday objects reaches us almost immediately. But as we look at things that are farther and farther away, it takes longer and longer for the light from them to travel to our eyes.

Light reaches the observer in 16 millionths of a second

The sound of thunder reaches the observer in about 15 seconds

Storm Cloud

Lightning Strike

An observer, 3 miles away, sees lightning flash about 15 seconds before hearing thunder

Light from the Sun, for example, takes slightly more than eight minutes to arrive at the Earth. Light from the brightest star in the night sky, Sirius, requires more than eight years to make the journey across a distance of about 25 **trillion*** miles. This means that we are seeing Sirius not as it is now, but as it was more than eight years ago! In the case of most stars in the night sky, their light has taken hundreds or even thousands of years to reach our eyes.

Everything we see and hear is from the past. In the case of a thunderstorm, the flash from a lightning strike reaches us about a million times faster than the sound of the thunder.

15

*Words in **bold type** are explained in the glossary at the end of this book.

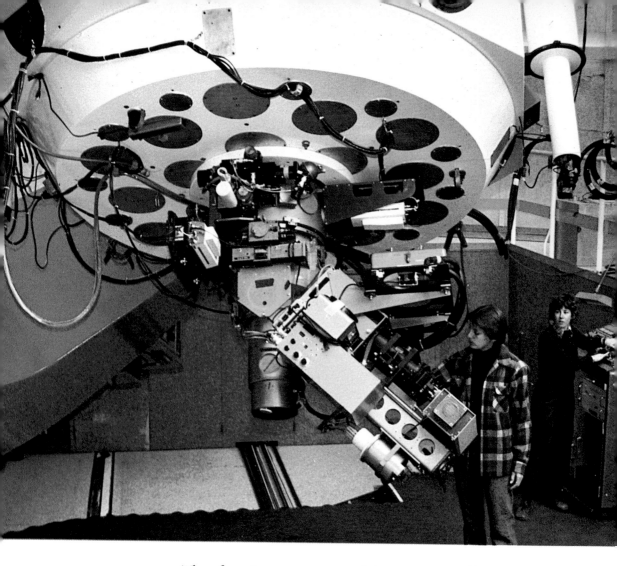

Instruments such
as this telescope at
Kitt Peak National
Observatory show
objects as they
were hundreds,
thousands, mil-
lions, and billions
of years in the
past.

The fact is, we see nothing as it really is. Everything you look at, even your own hand or the writing on this page, is as it was in the past. What is
more, the farther away you look, the farther back in
time you see. Here on Earth this effect is so tiny
that we are never aware of it. But for the astronomers studying the Universe, the effect is very
important, indeed. By gazing out into space
through giant telescopes, astronomers can look far
back in time. If they look at the most distant

objects yet discovered, they can see the Universe as it was about 15 **billion** years ago, not long after it was formed.

With the help of modern inventions, then, we can store sounds and pictures of events, and later replay them. By gazing more deeply into space, we can look farther and farther back into time. This means that devices such as cameras, video recorders, and telescopes are all "time machines" of a sort. And yet, they are useless for actually traveling into the past or for giving us any idea of what the future might be like.

To explore the past in person, or to see into the future, would be much more interesting. But it might also lead to some unusual and quite baffling problems.

Young people pretend they are astronauts inside a command module mockup at the U.S. Space and Rocket Center in Huntsville, Alabama. The mockup was used as a training device for astronauts preparing to go on missions to the moon.

It's Yesterday Once More

Any sensible explorer will prepare well before setting out on an adventure into the unknown. So, before looking at how real time travel might be achieved, we should consider the risks and problems that might be involved. Like Marty McFly in *Back to the Future*, we might find that trips into the past can affect the future in unexpected ways.

Imagine, for instance, you have just invented a vehicle that can transport you back to any date you wish. You dial a time 150 years ago, sit back in the pilot's seat, and pull back the starting lever. There is a blurred motion outside the cabin window. In just a few seconds, as measured by your own watch, you have hurtled back a century and a half.

Unfortunately, your time machine has landed on and squashed one of your ancestors. Had the accident not happened, this person would have become the father of your great-great-grandfather. But now history has been changed. A whole branch of your family has been destroyed. And worst of all, without that part of your family tree, you will not be born! Yet, here you are standing outside your time machine in the 1840s. How can this be?

Hurriedly climbing back into your machine, you reset the time dial to April 14, 1865. The destination

you choose is Ford's Theater, Washington, D.C. You arrive just minutes before John Wilkes Booth is due to slip into the private box of Abraham Lincoln and his wife to shoot the president. At least now you have a chance to make up for your earlier mistake. Quickly, you warn the police of the assassination attempt on Lincoln. Because of your action, the gunman is arrested, and Lincoln is not killed. But what will be the effect on world history?

20

Changing the Past

Even sending back objects rather than people into
the past could cause some strange problems. In one
short story, a professor invents a machine that can
transport a small brass cube back through time. He
tells his friend that at exactly three o'clock, he will
place a cube on the time machine's platform and
send it back five minutes into the past.

"Therefore," says the professor, "the
cube should, at five minutes before three,
vanish from my hand and appear on the
platform." And, sure enough, it does.

"See!" exclaims the professor. "Five
minutes before I shall place it there, it is
there!"

But now comes the interesting part of
the story. One of the professor's friends has a ques-
tion. What would happen, now that the box has made
its journey back through time, if the professor fails
to put the box on the time machine at three o'clock?
Fascinated, the professor decides to find out. It
proves to be a terrible mistake. In the story, at exactly
three o'clock, the professor, his friends, and the
whole Universe—except for the brass box—disappear!

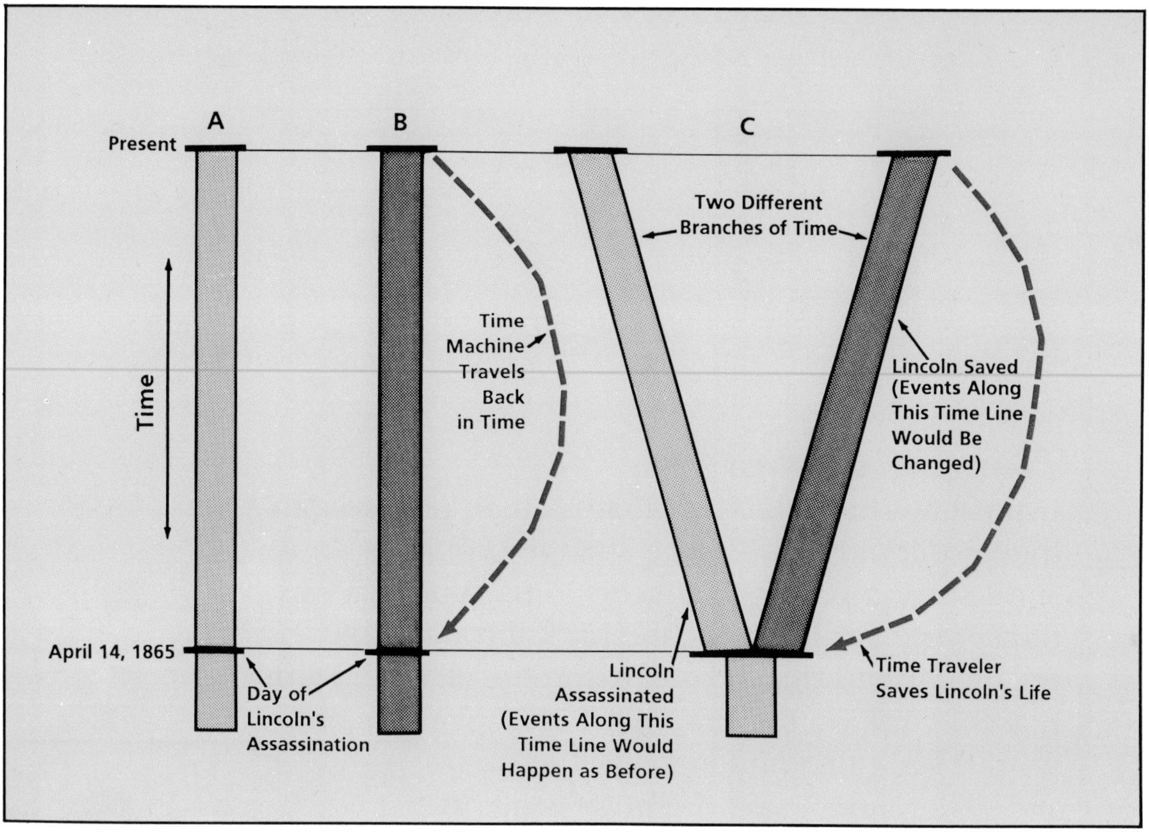
A
B
C
Present
Two Different
Branches of Time
Time
Time
Machine
Travels
Back
in Time
Lincoln Saved
(Events Along
This Time Line
Would Be
Changed)
April 14, 1865
Day of
Lincoln's
Assassination
Lincoln
Assassinated
(Events Along This
Time Line Would
Happen as Before)
Time Traveler
Saves Lincoln's Life

What would happen if a time traveler went back to April 14, 1865, and saved Lincoln's life? One possibility, as shown here, is that two futures would be created—one in which Lincoln was shot, and one in which he lived on.

When we start talking about time travel into the past, we encounter many logical problems such as the ones just mentioned. For this reason, some scientists believe that going back in time is not possible. Others argue that, if a time traveler did go into the past, it would cause a split in time. One branch of time would carry on as before. The other, with the time traveler in it, would contain differences because of the time traveler's actions.

According to this theory, if you went back to try to save Lincoln's life, you would create two different futures. In one, Lincoln would be shot and killed. In another, containing you and your time machine, he would live on.

Where Are All the Time Machines?

One of the strongest arguments that has been made against time travel could be called "the case of the missing time machines." In other words, if in the future time machines are invented, then why has no one seen any of them yet?

If time travel did become possible, it seems likely that thousands of people would want to take advantage of it. Time cruises could be offered to the age when wooly mammoths and sabre-toothed tigers still roamed the Earth. Other tourists might be more interested in seeing ancient Rome or Columbus setting sail for the New World. Surely, if time machines from the future had visited key moments in history, including our own time, someone would have spotted them by now.

Well, perhaps they have. It is possible, for instance, that some **UFOs**, or Unidentified Flying Objects, are time machines from the future. The chances of this being true are very, very small indeed. It is also possible that we cannot see these future time travelers or their machines. They may choose to keep themselves invisible to avoid changing history. In spite of the problems that it

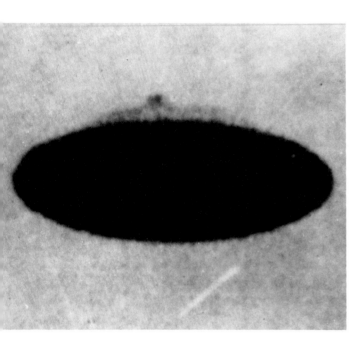

A photograph of a UFO, taken as part of a U.S. Air Force project.

seems to raise, time travel may be taking place.

Seeing Into the Future

Can some people see events before they actually happen? Is there a connection between the present and the future?

A large number of men, women, and children claim to have experienced **precognition**. This often takes the form of a dream in which a disaster is seen taking place, such as the crash of an aircraft. Later, the accident may occur just as in the dream. As with all such claims, it is very difficult to supply hard proof.

A second type of experience, which many of us have from time to time, is called **deja vu**. This is a sensation, lasting just a few seconds, that what is happening has occurred in exactly the same way before. Could it be that a future situation has been seen in a dream, forgotten, and then remembered only when it actually takes place? No one knows.

Finally, there is the mystery of **premonition**. This is the feeling many people say they have that something, perhaps very sad, happy, or important, is about to take place. More often than not, it involves members of the same family, and especially identical twins.

If precognition, deja vu, and premonition are real, rather than imagined, then scientists have a difficult problem. They must explain why human beings appear to be able to see into the future. Is there some "sixth sense," as yet undetected, that can reach back and forth in time? Or do future events send out ripples into the past that we can pick up, especially when we are asleep? Much more research is needed to find the answers.

But whether or not we can see future events, it is possible that someday people will be able to travel into the future. There are at least two ways, in theory, that human beings could use to journey far into the world of tomorrow.

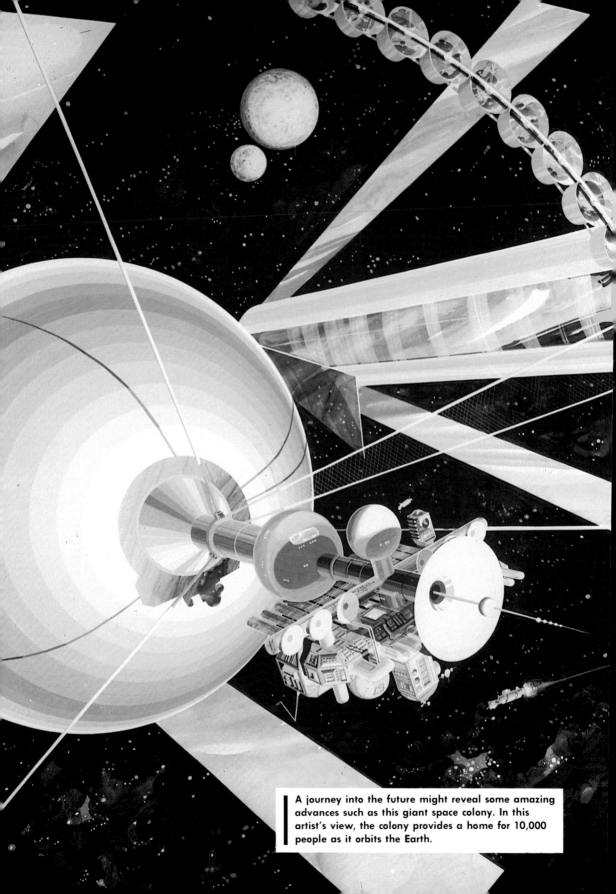

A journey into the future might reveal some amazing advances such as this giant space colony. In this artist's view, the colony provides a home for 10,000 people as it orbits the Earth.

Shortcuts to the Future

Within the last 100 years, the world has changed beyond all recognition. To someone from the year 1890, jet aircraft, television sets, computers, microwave ovens, and many other modern devices would seem like magic. A century ago, people traveled slowly by horse-drawn carriage. Today, they glide along freeways in cars at a mile a minute. Now people can pick up a phone and talk to someone almost anywhere on Earth. They can watch events in another country as they happen via signals transmitted by a satellite far out in space.

Given that change has come so quickly, imagine what things

may be like in the year 2100 or beyond. Perhaps, by then, people will have colonized other planets around the Sun. Or there may be computers that are more intelligent than human beings. The possibilities are endless, and we can scarcely begin to imagine them all.

Zooming into the future sounds like something only Marty McFly could do in his time-traveling sports car. Yet it is not as far-fetched as it seems.

The Long, Deep Sleep

Along with the rest of the Universe, we are all traveling into the future every instant of our lives. In time, we become older and die, which limits how far forward we can go. From the moment we are born, we have the chance to see, on average, about 75 years into the future. Some people are fortunate and live to be more than 100. But beyond that our only chance of survival is to slow or stop the normal process of aging.

Scientists already know that some very small animals can live much longer than usual by becoming dried out. **Tardigrades**, for instance, are small, squat creatures less than a twentieth of an inch in

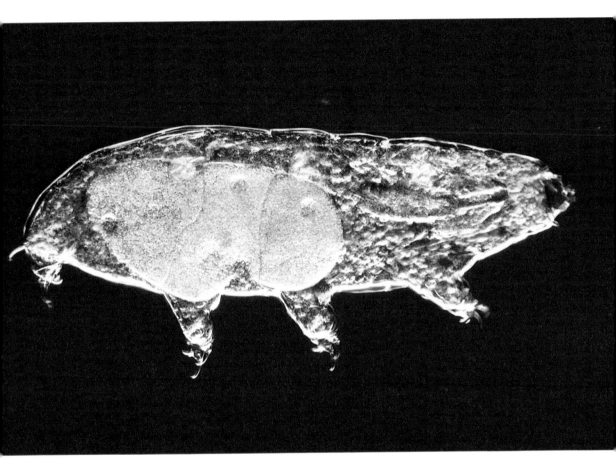

length with four pairs of legs. Normally, they live in films and pools of fresh water. But if the water dries up, so do the tardigrades. Humans would die if they lost more than one-fifth of the water in their bodies. Tardigrades can lose 99 percent of their body-water and still survive. In this parched condition, they can live for long periods of time. A tardigrade that is repeatedly dried out and revived can lengthen its life from a normal span of less than a year to about 60 years!

In a dried-out condition, a tardigrade can extend its life to as much as 60 times its normal life span.

Another way to extend life is to place it in a deep freeze. Researchers, for instance, have revived **bacteria** that became trapped in antarctic ice thousands of years ago. But would the same methods of lengthening life work with a person?

Drying out people and preserving them like tardigrades will not work. Humans will die if they lose that much body water. But the idea of freezing living people and reviving them at a later date is more reasonable. The main problem is that water expands when it freezes. Water is a major ingredient in all the **cells**, or tiny living units, of our bodies. If frozen, this water would tend to burst and kill every cell.

Despite such problems, several American companies already offer the unusual service of freezing dead bodies. The bodies are frozen so that in the future, doctors may have the opportunity to treat the conditions that caused the people to die. For now, reviving frozen human beings, whether dead or alive, is not possible. But in the years to come, new advances may help to make this technique work.

There is a better chance that we shall learn how to extend our lives using special medicines or

replacement body parts. Perhaps within your lifetime, human beings will live longer than they do today.

Time and Speed

Another way to travel into the future was discovered by the great German-American scientist Albert Einstein in the early 1900s. Einstein found that strange things happen to an object as it reaches very high speeds.

The key to understanding these unusual effects is the speed of light. Light moves 186,282 miles per second in empty space—the highest possible speed in the Universe. But, as Einstein first pointed out, the speed of light is always measured as 186,282 miles per second. Its speed stays the same whether a person or object is moving toward the source of the light or away from it!

This seems not to make sense compared to other

The famous physicist Albert Einstein demonstrates one of his scientific theories.

scientific measurements. For example, if you measured the speed of an oncoming car while driving down the freeway, the closing speed would be equal to your own speed plus that of the approaching vehicle. But that does not work in the case of light. Your own speed does not affect in the slightest the speed at which the light appears to be moving.

Starting from this simple, surprising fact, Einstein went on to produce an amazing theory. He realized that if the speed of light always remains the same, then other basic quantities such as time and length must vary. Previously, scientists had believed that time always flows at the same rate everywhere in the Universe. But Einstein proved that this is not

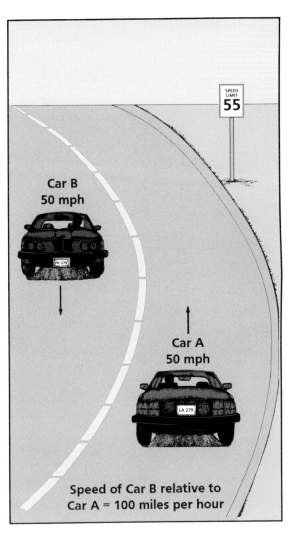

Car B
50 mph

Car A
50 mph

Speed of Car B relative to
Car A = 100 miles per hour

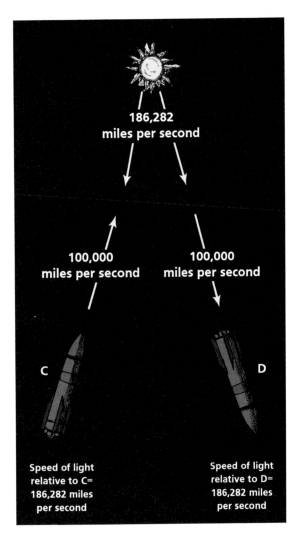

186,282
miles per second

100,000
miles per second

100,000
miles per second

C

D

Speed of light
relative to C=
186,282 miles
per second

Speed of light
relative to D=
186,282 miles
per second

true. In fact, for objects moving at high speed, time slows down!

According to the math behind Einstein's theory, the effects of time slowing down only become noticeable near to the speed of light. So far, no one has traveled as fast as one-thousandth of light-speed. Even the astronauts who went to the Moon reached a top speed of just 25,000 miles per hour. This is equal to seven miles per second, or about 26,000 times slower than light! The clocks aboard the

The speed of light is constant. To the driver of Car A, Car B seems to be approaching at 100 miles per hour. But the pilot of a high-speed spaceship would measure the speed of light to be the same whether the spaceship was moving toward the source of light, or away from it.

Time-Traveling Particles

It will be many years before spacecraft are built that can travel close to the speed of light. But Einstein's predictions about the strange slowing down of time at high speeds can already be tested today on much smaller objects.

Every day, the Earth is showered with tiny particles that come from far away in space. These particles, which are of various types, are known as cosmic rays. When cosmic rays strike the Earth's upper atmosphere, they give rise to other particles known as mesons.

Mesons have a lifetime of about two-millionths of a second. During that instant in time, they could normally cover about 2,000 feet. This is far short of the distance they would have to travel to reach the Earth's surface from the edge of space where they are created. Yet mesons, formed from collisions with cosmic rays, are detected on the ground! How can this be?

Mesons travel so fast that time slows down for them. Thus they have a much longer lifetime than normal. In other words, to a meson moving at near light-speed, the 25 miles it must travel to reach the Earth's surface seems like only a few hundred yards. The rate by which the meson's own time is slowed down, scientists have found, exactly matches the amount predicted by Einstein's theory.

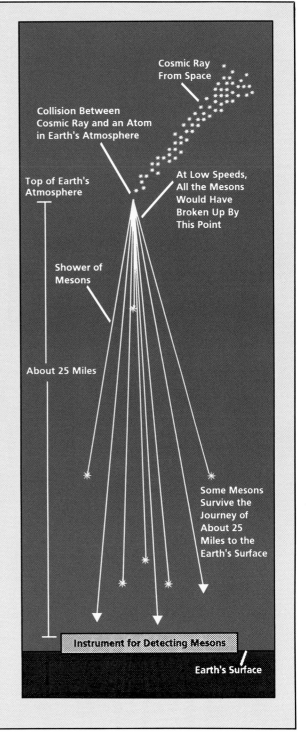

Cosmic Ray From Space

Collision Between Cosmic Ray and an Atom in Earth's Atmosphere

Top of Earth's Atmosphere

At Low Speeds, All the Mesons Would Have Broken Up By This Point

Shower of Mesons

About 25 Miles

Some Mesons Survive the Journey of About 25 Miles to the Earth's Surface

Instrument for Detecting Mesons

Earth's Surface

This Apollo astronaut, and others who traveled to the Moon, aged by very slightly less than if they had stayed on Earth.

Apollo spaceships did run slightly slower than clocks on Earth. Still, the astronauts aged only about one-thousandth of a second less than if they had not gone on the journey.

In years to come, though, it is likely that humans will build much faster space-craft. Indeed, they will have to if they hope to cross the vast distances to even the nearest stars within a crew's lifetime. Then, the effects predicted by Einstein will become much more important.

Lost in Time

The table on page 37 shows how much time would slow down for objects moving at various speeds. Traveling at 10 percent of light speed, or 18,628 miles per second, a spacecraft's time would not be slowed down by much. But at 90 percent of the speed of light, or 167,654 miles per second, time changes greatly. The crew members aboard such a spacecraft would age by less than half the amount than if they had stayed behind on Earth.

Imagine the situation, though, of a starship that can reach 99.999 percent of light speed. Traveling at

Einstein's Time-Slowing Effect

Time slows down as the speed of light is approached. This table shows how much time would slow, relative to clocks on Earth, for a spaceship traveling at various percentages of the speed of light.

For example, imagine a journey by a spaceship traveling at 95 percent of the speed of light. It lasts 10 years as measured by clocks on Earth. Then, using the table below, the travel time as measured by clocks aboard the spaceship would be 10 divided by 3.202, or 3.12 years. At 99 percent of light-speed, the spaceship's clocks would show that the journey lasted just 10 divided by 7.089, or 1.41 years.

Percentage of the speed of light (relative to Earth)	Amount by which time is slowed (relative to Earth)
0	1.000
10	1.005
20	1.021
30	1.048
40	1.091
50	1.155
60	1.250
70	1.400
80	1.667
90	2.294
95	3.202
99	7.089
99.9	22.361
99.999	223.607

this rate, the starship's crew would live 1 year for every 223 years that went by on Earth. Suppose the voyage lasted 10 years as measured by clocks on board the starships. Then when the crew returned to Earth, they would find themselves 2,230 years in the future! While they had been away, the world would have changed beyond their wildest dreams. It would be as if a group of ancient Greeks had been suddenly transported into the 1990s.

Yet who would want to make such a journey? Imagine that you could leap hundreds, thousands, or even millions of years into the future to see what fantastic developments had taken place. But time-traveling in a high-speed spaceship would allow you to go only one way. You would have to leave your homeland and time far behind, and you would be a stranger in a place far, far away. There would be no way to return to Earth. Yet there is one other way of traveling through time that might not have these problems. In theory, it would permit two-way voyages—both into the future and the past. But it would also mean flying into one of the strangest and most terrifying objects scientists have ever imagined.

In this artist's view, a future spaceship arrives at a strange world far away in space. If the spaceship traveled close to the speed of light, its crew would age much less than the people on Earth who did not make the superfast trip.

An artist imagines what the area in space around a black hole might look like.

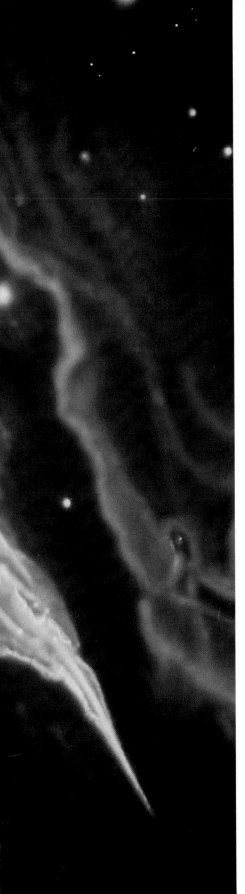

Black Holes and Time Tunnels

High in the sky on a clear fall evening is the star group of Cygnus the swan. It is not hard to find. Look for a large pattern of stars in the shape of a cross, or a swan in flight.

A map of the constellation Cygnus is shown on page 42. On the map, the end of the swan's tail is marked by a bright star called Deneb. Slightly ahead of Deneb are three stars in a line. They represent the swan's body and the tips of its wings. Finally, some distance away is a fifth, fairly bright star, Albireo. It marks the position of the great bird's head.

Now look halfway along the neck of the swan. There is a point

The constellation, or star group, of Cygnus the swan.

Deneb

Cygnus X-1

Albireo

on the map labeled Cygnus X-1. The next time you are outside on a clear, dark fall evening, locate Cygnus and gaze at the spot where Cygnus X-1 lies. Though you will not actually see anything, you will be looking at the exact point in space where scientists believe there may be a **black hole**.

Crushed Out of Sight

Black holes are popular subjects in films, as well as in many science fiction stories. But there is a good chance that black holes really exist in space. They are places where the pull of **gravity** is so strong that nothing, not even light, can escape from them. Once inside a black hole, you could never come back out the same way. However, it is possible that you could escape by a different route and arrive at a totally different part of the Universe. What is more, a journey into a black hole might transport you through time, either into the far future or the remote past.

How can black holes be made? They might be created by the explosion of very heavy stars. A star that weighs 20 or 30 times as much as the Sun can only shine brightly for a few million years. Then it blows itself apart. During this huge explosion, known as a **supernova**, all the top layers of the old star are blasted away into space at high speed. However, the **core**, or central part, of the star may remain whole.

In a normal, middle-aged star, such as the Sun, the core is the place where light and heat are made. Here the temperatures are incredibly hot—many millions of degrees. The outward pressure of this light and heat prevents the inward force of gravity from squeezing the core any smaller. For most of a star's life, these two great forces struggle against one another in an evenly matched game of tug-of-war. But in a dead star,

The Crab Nebula is the remains of a massive star that blew apart at the end of its life. Though the Crab Nebula does not contain a black hole, these strange objects may be found in the super-nova wreckage of some other giant stars.

there is no longer any light pressure to oppose gravity. As a result, the core is squeezed tighter and tighter and gets smaller and smaller.

When the average-sized stars, such as the Sun, reach the end of their lives, their cores shrink down to hot balls of squashed matter. These are called **white dwarfs**. Then another force, caused by particles of matter becoming too crowded together, stops gravity from crushing a white dwarf to an even smaller size.

44

In bigger, heavier stars, the force of gravity acting on the star's dead core is much stronger. Even after the supernova explosion has blown away much of the star's contents, the core that remains may be heavier than the Sun. If the core is more than three times as heavy as the Sun, nothing can prevent gravity from crushing the core smaller and smaller. From an original size of more than 20,000 miles across, the core is squashed in less than a tenth of a second to a ball only 25 miles across. At this stage, a tablespoonful of this matter would weigh the same as four billion full-grown elephants. But gravity squeezes it still smaller. In a fraction of a second, more than three sun's worth of star material becomes crammed into an incredibly tiny space. Now it may be no larger than the period at the end of this sentence.

45

Within a few miles of the totally crushed star, gravity is so strong that it will pull in anything that comes too close. And it will allow nothing to escape, not even a ray of light traveling at more than 186,000 miles per second. This region around the crushed star is completely black and invisible. That is why scientists call it a black hole.

The Mystery of Cygnus X-1

If black holes are black and invisible, then how can we ever know they are there? In fact, we cannot, unless there is something nearby that can be seen and upon which the black hole has a noticeable effect. This is the case with Cygnus X-1.

From observations made by instruments in space, scientists have discovered that huge amounts of **X rays**—rays that carry a great deal of energy—are coming from the direction of Cygnus X-1. They have also found that a **binary star** lies in the same position as the source of the X rays. A binary star consists of two stars that are circling around each other. One of these stars is much bigger and brighter than the Sun, but it can only be seen through a large telescope because it is so far away. Astrono-

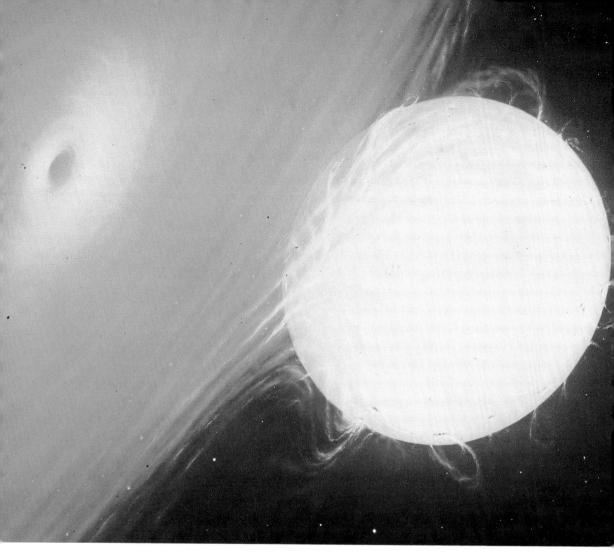

mers know it is there because of the "wobbles" it causes in the movement of its giant neighbor.

From the extent of the wobbles, astronomers think the dark star in Cygnus X-1 must weigh from five to eight times as much as the Sun. This fact alone suggests that it is likely to be a black hole. But the X rays offer still stronger evidence. Careful studies of the X rays have revealed that they are almost certainly coming from a whirlpool of extremely hot gas. This gas, scientists believe, has been stripped

An artist imagines how the black hole in Cygnus X-1 might look as it strips away gas from a nearby, giant star.

47

away from the bright, giant star by the gravitational pull of a nearby black hole. Just before it disappears down the black hole, the gas is heated to more than 18 million °F. At that superhot temperature, it gives off an intense X-ray glow.

Into the Black Hole
Even before scientists found signs of real black holes in the Universe, they had studied the mathematics of what black holes might be like inside. According to their theories, black holes may be like the entrances of tunnels that join different regions of space and time. These strange tunnels are called

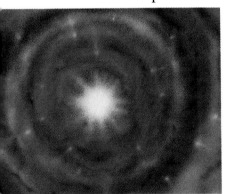

wormholes. At the end of a wormhole is an exit known as a **white hole**. By going into a black hole, traveling along its wormhole, and then coming out the white hole at the other end, a spacecraft might be able to leap across huge distances of space and millions of years in time.

But two British scientists, Stephen Hawking and Roger Penrose, pointed out some problems with this wonderful way to travel. For one thing, there seems to be an energy barrier

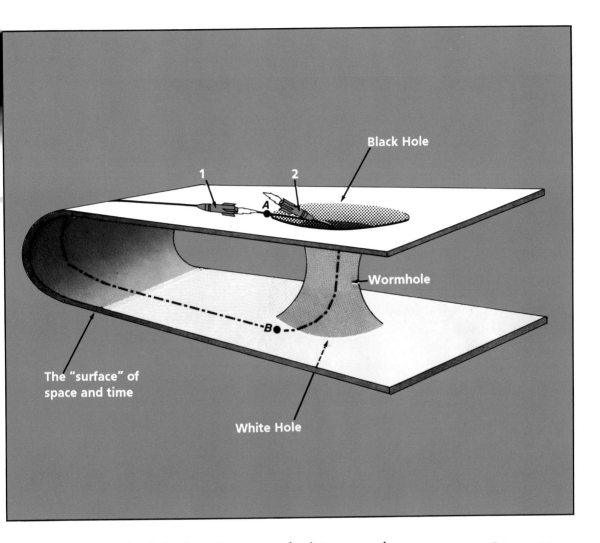

Black Hole

1

2

A

Wormhole

The "surface" of
space and time

B

White Hole

inside a black hole. No normal object, such as a
spacecraft, could pass through this barrier without
being torn to bits. The two scientists identified a second major problem. It appears that the wormhole
tunnel would instantly squeeze shut if a piece of
matter tried to move along it.

However, in 1988, new results were produced by
researchers Michael Morris, Kip Thorne, and Ulvi Yurtsever at the California Institute of Technology. These
showed that a wormhole might be kept open with

To travel from a
point in space and
time A to another
point in space and
time B, Spaceship 1
takes an ordinary
route around the
Universe. Space-
craft 2, though,
takes a shortcut
using a wormhole.
If B lies farther
back in time than
A, then the jour-
ney could only be
made through the
wormhole.

the help of two round plates that carried a charge of electricity. The plates would be located on either side of the "throat" leading into the wormhole. Results from even more recent research have shown that objects entering a spinning black hole might also be able to travel through time.

Yet, just because something is possible in theory does not mean it will quickly, or ever, become fact. We are still not certain that black holes exist. The evidence for them, though, is strong. If they do exist, then the nearest one is likely to be many trillions of miles away. Cygnus X-1 is about 10,000 **light-years** from Earth. One light-year is the distance that light travels in a year, or about 6 trillion miles. Cygnus X-1, then, lies about 60 thousand trillion miles away!

It is possible that there are closer black holes to Earth that we have not yet found. If they are not members of binary star systems, then they would be extremely hard to detect. Still, it would be surprising if there were a black hole similar to Cygnus X-1 that was closer than a few hundred light-years to the Sun. At such a distance, it would be very difficult to reach such an object. And it would be even harder to use it as a time machine.

50

Scientists do not know how many black holes may exist among the trillions of stars in the Universe.

Black Holes, Large and Small

Much larger black holes, weighing millions or even billions of times as much as the Sun, are thought to lie in the center of **galaxies**. Galaxies are huge collections of stars arranged in spiral, round, oval, or irregular shapes. We live in a galaxy called the Milky Way. To explain the unusual amount of energy coming from the middle of large galaxies, scientists have proposed the idea of "supermassive" black holes. But these would lie even farther from Earth than black holes that formed from neighboring stars.

There may also be mini black holes. These may be smaller than a pea but with the **mass**, or amount of matter, of a mountain. It is also possible that scientists will someday be able to create their own tiny black holes in the laboratory. They might do this by directing extremely intense, pure beams of light into a tiny pellet of matter. If enough energy could be focused onto the pellet at one time, it would collapse to form a black hole so small that it could only be seen under a microscope.

But there is a problem with this plan. Small black holes would tend to rip apart any object that was sent into them. This would happen because the pull of gravity on anything approaching a mini black hole would be much greater at the front of the object than at the back.

In the case of a very large, massive black hole, the difference in gravitational pull across an approaching object would be much less. The supermassive black holes that may occupy the center of some galaxies also appear to be the only kind that human beings might be able to enter and survive.

Beyond the Light Barrier

According to Einstein's Special Theory of Relativity, no object can reach the speed of light. As an object goes faster, its mass increases. That makes it harder and harder to boost its speed further. To reach the speed of light, even a particle that started out with a tiny mass would require more energy than there is in the whole Universe.

Einstein's theory, though, does not say that faster-than-light particles cannot exist. It only says that if there are such particles, known as tachyons, then they can never travel at or less than light speed.

If tachyons did turn out to be real, they would behave in a very strange way. They would travel backward in time! This is another prediction of Einstein's theory. Any object that travels faster than light would seem to us to be moving into the past. As a result, a tachyon could be de-

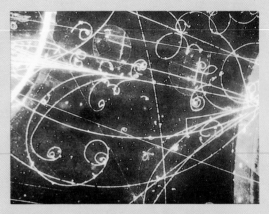

This greatly magnified view shows the tracks made by the collisions of very tiny particles.

tected by an instrument before the event in which it was actually formed. On the practical side, tachyons might make possible an unusual kind of telephone. On this phone, calls could be sent into the past! So far, despite searches carried out by various groups of researchers, no real tachyon has yet been found.

The Prospects for Time Travel

Could you then build a time machine? With devices such as cameras and video recorders, it is already possible to review events from the past. Researchers are also making progress in learning how humans age and how the aging process might be slowed down. Perhaps within 20 or 30 years, there will be methods to allow people to live longer. If so, they will see much more of the future.

Other forms of time travel will probably take longer to develop. It is unlikely that there will be any crew-carrying spaceships that can fly close to the speed of light by the end of the twenty-first century. But such craft will be built. Then human beings who travel to the stars will go on journeys through time. They will leap hundreds, thousands, or even millions of years into the future during their own lifetimes.

Scientists today do not know if black holes will ever be used as a means to jump instantly into the remote past or future. The technical problems to be overcome, even if such journeys are possible, are among the most difficult imaginable. Yet the people who lived a century ago might have thought of human missions to the Moon in the same way.

Someday, in some form, the human race is likely to build a machine that can swiftly travel through time. Where that will lead us to, no one yet knows.

Hands On

Launch your own capsule on a journey through time. Containing objects and information about life today, it will travel into the future to be opened by someone perhaps late in the 21st century.

Your time capsule should be an airtight container made of material such as plastic that will not rot or rust. An ice-cream container, for example, would work well.

Choose carefully the items you want to send into the future. Imagine that you had just found a time capsule that had been made many years ago. What kinds of things would you hope to find inside—newspaper clippings, photographs, small toys, wrappings from food cans and packages? Use these ideas for your own capsule. Include details of your school, friends, important news stories of the year, current world records in sports, results of the last presidential election, family photographs with notes on the back, a picture of yourself, and clippings from a mail order catalog. You could also record a cassette tape of sounds in your everyday-life— people talking, traffic and airport noise, TV programs, and popular songs. Next, place inside any small objects that you think might prove interesting to the people of the future.

Pack all the items neatly into the time capsule, ensuring that anything breakable is deep inside and well padded. Press the lid on firmly and, if you wish, seal it with masking tape. Write any instructions, such as "Do not open until the year 2090," on the outside. Finally, "launch" the time capsule by burying it in the ground or hiding it in the attic of your house.

Glossary

bacteria—very small, single-celled plants that exist in large numbers almost everywhere on Earth

billion—a thousand million; written as 1,000,000,000

binary star—two stars that are close together and circle around one another; according to some estimates, roughly half of all stars are members of binary systems

black hole—a region of space in which the pull of gravity is so strong that nothing, not even light, can escape. A black hole may form from the squashed remains of a very heavy star after the parts of the star have been blown away in a supernova explosion

cell—the smallest living unit making up an animal or plant. Cells are usually too small to be seen without the help of a microscope. They come in many forms and serve many different purposes. Examples include red blood cells, bone cells, and brain cells

core—in a star, the extremely hot region in the middle where the star produces its light and heat

deja vu—a French expression meaning "already seen;" deja vu is the name for the strange feeling people have that what is happening has happened once before

galaxy—a very large collection of between a few billion and a few hundred billion stars. The galaxy in which we live, the Milky Way Galaxy, is spiral in shape, contains about 200 billion stars, and measures more than 100,000 light-years across

gravity—a force exerted by any object that has mass. The Earth's gravity is the force that prevents the atmosphere, and people, from floating away into space

light-year—a unit used by astronomers to measure distances in the Universe. It is the distance that light, traveling 186,282 miles per second, covers in a year. One light-year equals 5.85 trillion miles

mass—mass can be thought of in two ways. It is a measure of the amount of matter in an object. Mass is also a measure of how hard it is to make an object move or make it move in a different way

precognition—the supposed ability of some people to be able to know what is going to happen or to sense clearly certain events in the future. It can take various forms, from "fortune telling" to dreaming about disasters before they occur

premonition—similar to precognition, but more of a vague feeling about the future than certain knowledge. There is still not enough evidence to show whether premonition and precognition are real or not

supernova—there are two types of supernovas. The one discussed in this book involves the explosion of an old, very massive type of star known as a supergiant. One of the possible results of a supernova is a black hole

tardigrade—a tiny, water-dwelling creature that can survive when most of the water in its body is lost. This allows the tardigrade to live through periods of drought and then become active again when water returns to its surroundings

trillion—a million million; written as 1,000,000,000,000

UFO—"Unidentified Flying Object." A UFO is any object seen in the sky for which there is no immediate explanation. Although many UFOs do turn out simply to be airplanes, bright stars or planets, or unusual clouds, a small number remain unexplained

white dwarf—the type of object that an average-sized star like the Sun becomes after it stops producing light and heat in its core. Most white dwarfs are from one to three times the size of the Earth

white hole—in theory, possibly the other end of a black hole. Instead of being like a whirlpool that sucks everything into it that comes too close, a white hole would look like a geyser in space from which matter and light would gush out

wormhole—in theory, a sort of tunnel that connects a black hole to some other region of space and time. Wormholes may or may not exist. If they do, they might be like subways connecting different parts of our own universe or even other universes.

X rays—rays that are similar to ordinary light but which carry much more energy. X rays may be produced in a variety of ways in space. As a gas, one of these becomes heated to millions of degrees

Index

Back to the Future, 4, 19
bacteria, 21-22
binary stars, 46-47, 50
black holes: Cygnus X-1, 41, 42, 46, 47,50; supermassive, 52, 53; theories about, 42, 46, 47-48, 50, 52, 53, 55
calendars, 9
cells, 30
changing the past, 4, 19-22
Cygnus X-1. *See* black holes
deja vu, 24
Einstein, Albert, 31, 34, 35, 37, 54
extending life: by drying out, 29-31; by freezing, 38
galaxies, 52
gravity, 42, 43, 44, 45, 46, 48, 53
Greenwich Mean Time, 13
Hawking, Stephen, 48
light: pressure of, 43-44; speed of, 14-15, 31-32, 33, 36, 54
light-years, 50
Lincoln, Abraham, 20
McFly, Marty, 7, 19, 28
mass, 53
mesons, 35
Morris, Michael, 49
Penrose, Roger, 48

photography, 10
precognition, 24
premonition, 25
sound, 10, 14
speed, 31-32, 33, 37
stars: Albireo, 41; binary, 46-47; cores of, 43, 44, 45; Deneb, 41; life of, 43-44; Sirius, 15; Sun, 15, 28, 44, 45; white dwarfs, 44
supernova, 43
tachyons, 54
tardigrades, 28-29
Theory of Relativity, 32, 54
Thorne, Kip, 49
time: control over, 7; rate of, 31, 32-33, 35, 36, 37, 39; ripples, 25; splitting of, 19, 20, 21, 22-23
time machines: black holes as, 48-50; theories about, 4, 19-20, 21-22, 23, 53-54; *The Time Machine*, 4
UFOs, 23
video recorders, 12, 17
Wells, H.G., 4
white dwarfs: *See* stars
white holes, 48
wormholes, 48, 49, 50
X rays, 46, 47, 48
Yurtsever, Ulvi, 49